Inflation and Unemployment:

The New Dimension of Politics

The 1976 Alfred Nobel Memorial Lecture

MILTON FRIEDMAN

Nobel Laureate 1976

Published by
THE INSTITUTE OF ECONOMIC AFFAIRS
1977

First published May 1977

by

THE INSTITUTE OF ECONOMIC AFFAIRS

© The Nobel Foundation 1977

ISSN 0073–909X

SBN 255 36096–7

Printed in Great Britain by

TONBRIDGE PRINTERS LTD, TONBRIDGE, KENT

Set in Monotype Plantin

Contents

[3]

Preface

THE *Occasional Papers* are intended to make essays and addresses of outstanding importance accessible to a wider readership than that to which they were originally addressed. The 50 so far have included *Papers* by some of Britain's, and the world's, leading economists but also some important *Papers* by less well-known thinkers.

The Institute is glad to make available to its readers, earlier than published elsewhere, a second Nobel Memorial Lecture. The first, delivered by Professor F. A. Hayek in Sweden in December 1974, was published in *Full Employment at Any Price ?*, Occasional Paper 45, in 1975. The second, by Professor Milton Friedman, was delivered in Stockholm in December 1976. The version here is the original spoken lecture, reproduced verbatim.

The theme is the one with which Professor Friedman has made his most original and far-reaching contribution to economics: the relationship between inflation and unemployment and in particular the processes by which control of the quantity of money influences prices and production. And, in addition to the most up-to-date refinement of these relationships in the light of monetary theory and history which have appeared in his recent writings in the USA and in IEA *Papers*, [1] Professor Friedman adds a discussion of the new dimension: the repercussions of the economics of politics.

The subject is of fundamental importance to economists and to the British people in particular, who have suffered more than most Western peoples from the simultaneous expansion of inflation and unemployment. In view of the difficulty of the subject and the closely argued economic analysis, an attempt at a child's guide has been made in the numbered summary on the back and inside back covers.

April 1977   ARTHUR SELDON

---

[1] *The Counter-Revolution in Monetary Theory* (the first Wincott Memorial Lecture), 1970; *Inflation: Causes, Consequences, Cures* (the proceedings of a Seminar), 1974; *Unemployment versus Inflation?* (IEA Lecture), 1975. The IEA has also published *Monetary Correction*, 1974, and *From Galbraith to Economic Freedom*, 1977.

[4]

The Author

MILTON FRIEDMAN was born in 1912 in New York City and graduated from Rutgers before taking MA at Chicago and PhD at Columbia. From 1935-37 he worked for the US National Resources Committee, from 1937-40 for the National Bureau of Economic Research, and from 1941-43 for the US Treasury.

Since 1946 Friedman has taught at the University of Chicago, where he is now the Paul Snowden Russell Distinguished Service Professor of Economics. He has taught also at the universities of Minnesota, Wisconsin, and Columbia, as well as lecturing at universities throughout the world from Cambridge to Tokyo. Since 1946 he has also been on the research staff of the National Bureau of Economic Research, and, from December 1976, a Senior Research Fellow at the Hoover Institution of Stanford University.

He is known to a wider audience as an advocate of a volunteer army (in place of the US draft), reverse income tax (in place of partial or universalist poverty programmes), monetary policy and floating exchange rates. He is the acknowledged head of the 'Chicago School' which specialises in the empirical testing of policy propositions derived from market analysis. Professor Friedman was awarded the 1976 Nobel Prize in Economic Sciences.

Among his best known books are *Essays in Positive Economics* (Chicago, 1953), *Studies in the Quantity Theory of Money* (edited by Friedman, Chicago, 1956), *A Theory of the Consumption Function* (Princeton, 1957), *Capitalism and Freedom* (Chicago, 1962), (with Anna J. Schwartz) *A Monetary History of the United States, 1867-1960* (Princeton, 1963), and *The Optimum Quantity of Money* (Aldine, Chicago, and Macmillan, London, 1969). The IEA has published his Wincott Memorial Lecture, *The Counter-Revolution in Monetary Theory* (Occasional Paper 33, 1970, 3rd impression 1974), *Monetary Correction* (Occasional Paper 41, 2nd impression 1974), his contributions to *Inflation: Causes, Consequences, Cures* (IEA Readings No. 14, 1974, 2nd impression 1975), *Unemployment versus Inflation?: An Evaluation of the Phillips Curve* (Occasional Paper 44, 3rd impression 1977), and *From Galbraith to Economic Freedom* (Occasional Paper 49, 2nd impression 1977).

Acknowledgments

I am much indebted for helpful comments on the first draft of this *Paper* to Gary Becker, Karl Brunner, Phillip Cagan, Robert Gordon, Arnold Harberger, Harry G. Johnson, S. Y. Lee, James Lothian, Robert E. Lucas, David Meiselman, Allan Meltzer, José Scheinkman, Theodore W. Schultz, Anna J. Schwartz, Larry Sjaastad, George J. Stigler, Sven-Ivan Sundqvist, and participants in the Money and Banking Workshop of the University of Chicago.

I am deeply indebted also to my wife, Rose Director Friedman, who took part in every stage of the preparation of the *Paper*, and to my secretarial assistant, Gloria Valentine, for performance above and beyond the call of duty.

M.F.

NOBEL LECTURE
Inflation and Unemployment:
The New Dimension of Politics
MILTON FRIEDMAN
Nobel Laureate 1976

WHEN THE Bank of Sweden established the prize for Economic Science in memory of Alfred Nobel (1968), there doubtless was – as there doubtless still remains – widespread scepticism among both scientists and the broader public about the appropriateness of treating economics as parallel to physics, chemistry, and medicine. These are regarded as 'exact sciences' in which objective, cumulative, definitive knowledge is possible. Economics, and its fellow social sciences, are regarded more nearly as branches of philosophy than of science properly defined, enmeshed with values at the outset because they deal with human behaviour. Do not the social sciences, in which scholars are analysing the behaviour of themselves and their fellow men, who are in turn observing and reacting to what the scholars say, require fundamentally different methods of investigation than the physical and biological sciences? Should they not be judged by different criteria?

I

SOCIAL AND NATURAL SCIENCES

I HAVE never myself accepted this view. I believe that it reflects a misunderstanding not so much of the character and possibilities of social science as of the character and possibilities of natural science. In both, there is no 'certain' substantive knowledge; only tentative hypotheses that can never be 'proved', but can only fail to be rejected, hypotheses in which we may have more or less confidence, depending on such features as the breadth of experience they encompass relative to their own complexity and relative to alternative hypotheses, and the number of occasions on which they have escaped possible rejection. In both social and natural sciences, the body of positive knowledge grows by the failure of a tentative hypothesis to predict phenomena the hypo-

[7]

thesis professes to explain; by the patching up of that hypothesis until someone suggests a new hypothesis that more elegantly or simply embodies the troublesome phenomena, and so on *ad infinitum.* In both, experiment is sometimes possible, sometimes not (witness meteorology). In both, no experiment is ever completely controlled, and experience often offers evidence that is the equivalent of controlled experiment. In both, there is no way to have a self-contained closed system or to avoid interaction between the observer and the observed. The Gödel theorem in mathematics, the Heisenberg uncertainty principle in physics, the self-fulfilling or self-defeating prophecy in the social sciences all exemplify these limitations.

Of course, the different sciences deal with different subject matter, have different bodies of evidence to draw on (for example, introspection is a more important source of evidence for social than for natural sciences), find different techniques of analysis most useful, and have achieved differential success in predicting the phenomena they are studying. But such differences are as great among, say, physics, biology, medicine, and meteorology as between any of them and economics.

Even the difficult problem of separating value-judgements from scientific judgements is not unique to the social sciences. I well recall a dinner at a Cambridge University college when I was sitting between a fellow economist and R. A. Fisher, the great mathematical statistician and geneticist. My fellow economist told me about a student he had been tutoring on labour economics, who, in connection with an analysis of the effect of trade unions, remarked, 'Well surely, Mr. X (another economist of a different political persuasion) would not agree with that'. My colleague regarded this experience as a terrible indictment of economics because it illustrated the impossibility of a value-free positive economic science. I turned to Sir Ronald and asked whether such an experience was indeed unique to social science. His answer was an impassioned 'no', and he proceeded to tell one story after another about how accurately he could infer views in genetics from political views.

One of my great teachers, Wesley C. Mitchell, impressed on me the basic reason why scholars have every incentive to pursue a value-free science, whatever their values and however strongly they may wish to spread and promote them. In order to recommend a course of action to achieve an objective, we must first know whether that course of action will in fact promote the objective. Positive scientific knowledge that enables us to predict the consequences of a possible course of action is clearly a prerequisite for the normative judgement whether that course of action is desirable. The Road to Hell is paved with good intentions, precisely because of the neglect of this rather obvious point.

This point is particularly important in economics. Many countries around the world are today experiencing socially destructive inflation, abnormally high unemployment, misuse of economic resources, and in some cases, the suppression of human freedom not because evil men deliberately sought to achieve these results, nor because of differences in values among their citizens, but because of erroneous judgements about the consequences of government measures: errors that at least in principle are capable of being corrected by the progress of positive economic science.

Rather than pursue these ideas in the abstract [I have discussed the methodological issues more fully in (1)], I shall illustrate the positive scientific character of economics by discussing a particular economic issue that has been a major concern of the economics profession throughout the post-war period; namely, the relation between inflation and unemployment. This issue is an admirable illustration because it has been a controversial political issue throughout the period, yet the drastic change that has occurred in accepted professional views was produced primarily by the scientific response to experience that contradicted a tentatively accepted hypothesis – precisely the classical process for the revision of a scientific hypothesis.

I cannot give here an exhaustive survey of the work that has been done on this issue or of the evidence that has led to the revision of the hypothesis. I shall be able only to skim the surface in the hope of conveying the flavour of that work and that evidence and of indicating the major items requiring further investigation.

Professional controversy about the relation between inflation and unemployment has been intertwined with controversy about the relative role of monetary, fiscal, and other factors in influencing aggregate demand. One issue deals with how a change in aggregate nominal demand, however produced, works itself out through changes in employment and price levels; the other, with the factors accounting for the changes in aggregate nominal demand.

The two issues are closely related. The effects of a change in aggregate nominal demand on employment and price levels may not be independent of the source of the change, and conversely, the effect of monetary, fiscal, or other forces on aggregate nominal demand may depend on how employment and price levels react. A full analysis will clearly have to treat the two issues jointly. Yet there is a considerable measure of independence between them. To a first approximation, the effects on employment and price levels may depend only on the magnitude of the change in aggregate nominal demand, not on its source. On both issues, professional opinion today is very different than it was just after World War II because experience contradicted tentatively accepted hypotheses. Either issue could therefore serve to illustrate my main thesis. I have chosen to deal with only one in order to keep this lecture within reasonable bounds. I have chosen to make that one the relation between inflation and unemployment, because recent experience leaves me less satisfied with the adequacy of my earlier work on that issue than with the adequacy of my earlier work on the forces producing changes in aggregate nominal demand.

II

STAGE I: NEGATIVELY SLOPING PHILLIPS CURVE

PROFESSIONAL analysis of the relation between inflation and unemployment has gone through two stages since the end of World War II and is now entering a third. The first stage was the acceptance of a hypothesis associated with the name of A. W. Phillips that there is a stable negative relation between the level of unemployment and the rate of change of wages – high levels of unemployment being accompanied by falling wages, low levels of unemployment by rising wages (24). The wage change in turn was linked to price change by allowing for the secular increase in productivity and treating the excess of price over wage cost as given by a roughly constant mark-up factor.

Figure 1 illustrates this hypothesis, where I have followed the standard practice of relating unemployment directly to price change, short-circuiting the intermediate step through wages.

This relation was widely interpreted as a causal relation that

Rate of price change

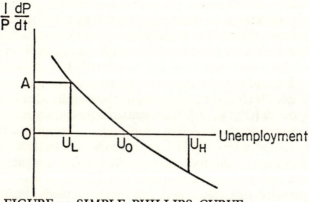

FIGURE 1: SIMPLE PHILLIPS CURVE

offered a stable trade-off to policy-makers. They could choose a low unemployment target, such as U_L. In that case they would have to accept an inflation rate of A. There would remain the problem of choosing the measures (monetary, fiscal, perhaps other) that would produce the level of aggregate nominal demand required to achieve U_L, but if that were done, there need be no concern about maintaining that combination of unemployment and inflation. Alternatively, the policy-makers could choose a low inflation rate or even deflation as their target. In that case they would have to reconcile themselves to higher unemployment: U_O for zero inflation, U_H for deflation.

Economists then busied themselves with trying to extract the relation depicted in Figure 1 from evidence for different countries and periods, to eliminate the effect of extraneous disturbances, to clarify the relation between wage change and price change, and so on. In addition, they explored social gains and losses from inflation on the one hand and unemployment on the other, in order to facilitate the choice of the 'right' trade-off.

Unfortunately for this hypothesis, additional evidence failed to conform to it. Empirical estimates of the Phillips curve relation were unsatisfactory. More important, the inflation rate that appeared to be consistent with a specified level of unemployment did not remain fixed: in the circumstances of the post-World War II period, when governments everywhere were seeking to promote 'full employment', it tended in any one country to rise over time and to vary sharply among countries. Looked at the other way, rates of inflation that had earlier been associated with low levels of unemployment were experienced along with high levels of unemployment. The phenomenon of simultaneous high inflation and high unemployment increasingly forced itself on public and professional notice, receiving the unlovely label of 'stagflation'.

Some of us were sceptical from the outset about the validity of a stable Phillips curve, primarily on theoretical rather than empirical grounds [(2), (3), (4)]. What mattered for employment, we argued, was not wages in dollars or pounds or kronor but real wages – what the wages would buy in goods and services. Low unemployment would, indeed, mean pressure for a higher real wage – but real wages could be higher even if nominal wages were lower, provided that prices were still lower. Similarly, high unemployment would, indeed, mean pressure for a lower real wage – but real wages could be lower, even if nominal wages were higher, provided prices were still higher.

There is no need to assume a stable Phillips curve in order to explain the apparent tendency for an acceleration of inflation to reduce unemployment. That can be explained by the impact of *unanticipated* changes in nominal demand on markets characterised by (implicit or explicit) long-term commitments with respect to both capital and labour. Long-term labour commitments can be explained by the cost of acquiring information by employers about employees and by employees about alternative employment opportunities plus the specific human capital that makes an employee's value to a particular employer grow over time and exceed his value to other potential employers.

Only surprises matter. If everyone anticipated that prices would rise at, say, 20 per cent a year, then this anticipation would be embodied in future wage (and other) contracts, real wages would then behave precisely as they would if everyone anticipated no price rise, and there would be no reason for the 20 per cent rate of inflation to be associated with a different level of unemployment than a zero rate. An unanticipated change is very different, especially in the presence of long-term commitments – themselves partly a result of the imperfect knowledge whose effect they enhance and spread over time. Long-term commitments mean, first, that there is not instantaneous market clearing (as in markets for perishable foods) but only a lagged adjustment of both prices and quantity to changes in demand or supply (as in the house-rental market); second, that commitments entered into depend not only on current observable prices, but also on the prices expected to prevail throughout the term of the commitment.

III

STAGE 2: THE NATURAL RATE HYPOTHESIS

PROCEEDING ALONG these lines, we [in particular, E. S. Phelps and myself (4), (22), (23)] developed an alternative hypothesis that distinguished between the short-run and long-run effects of unanticipated changes in aggregate nominal demand. Start from some initial stable position and let there be, for example, an un-anticipated acceleration of aggregate nominal demand. This will come to each producer as an unexpectedly favourable demand for his product. In an environment in which changes are always occurring in the relative demand for different goods, he will not know whether this change is special to him or pervasive. It will be rational for him to interpret it as at least partly special and to react to it, by seeking to produce more to sell at what he now perceives to be a higher than expected market price for future output. He will be willing to pay higher nominal wages than he had been willing to pay before in order to attract additional workers. The real wage that matters to him is the wage in terms of the price of his product, and he perceives that price as higher than before. A higher nominal wage can therefore mean a lower *real* wage as perceived by him.

To workers, the situation is different: what matters to them is the purchasing power of wages not over the particular good they produce but over all goods in general. Both they and their employers are likely to adjust more slowly their perception of prices in general – because it is more costly to acquire information about that – than their perception of the price of the particular good they produce. As a result, a rise in nominal wages may be perceived by workers as a rise in real wages and hence call forth an increased supply, at the same time that it is perceived by employers as a fall in real wages and hence calls forth an increased offer of jobs. Expressed in terms of the average of perceived future prices, real wages are lower; in terms of the perceived future average price, real wages are higher.

[13]

But this situation is temporary: let the higher rate of growth of aggregate nominal demand and of prices continue, and perceptions will adjust to reality. When they do, the initial effect will disappear, and then even be reversed for a time as workers and employers find themselves locked into inappropriate contracts. Ultimately, employment will be back at the level that prevailed before the assumed unanticipated acceleration in aggregate nominal demand.

This alternative hypothesis is depicted in Figure 2. Each negatively sloping curve is a Phillips curve like that in Figure 1 except that it is for a particular anticipated or perceived rate of inflation, defined as the perceived average rate of price change, *not* the average of perceived rates of individual price change (the order of the curves would be reversed for the second concept). Start from point E and let the rate of inflation for whatever reason move from A to B and stay there. Unemployment would initially decline to U_L at point F, moving along the curve defined for an anticipated rate of inflation $\left(\frac{1}{P}\frac{dP}{dt}\right)$* of A. As anticipations adjusted, the short-run curve would move upward, ultimately to the curve defined for an anticipated inflation rate of B. Concurrently unemployment would move gradually over from F to G. [For a fuller discussion, see (5).]

This analysis is, of course, over-simplified. It supposes a single unanticipated change, whereas, of course, there is a continuing

Rate of inflation

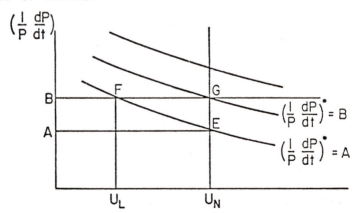

FIGURE 2: EXPECTATIONS – ADJUSTED PHILLIPS CURVE

stream of unanticipated changes; it does not deal explicitly with lags, or with overshooting; or with the process of formation of anticipations. But it does highlight the key points: what matters is not inflation *per se*, but unanticipated inflation; there is no stable trade-off between inflation and unemployment; there is a 'natural rate of unemployment' (U_N), which is consistent with the real forces and with accurate perceptions; unemployment can be kept below that level only by an accelerating inflation; or above it, only by accelerating deflation.

The 'natural rate of unemployment', a term I introduced to parallel Knut Wicksell's 'natural rate of interest', is not a numerical constant but depends on 'real' as opposed to monetary factors – the effectiveness of the labour market, the extent of competition or monopoly, the barriers or encouragements to working in various occupations, and so on.

For example, the natural rate has clearly been rising in the United States for two major reasons. First, women, teenagers, and part-time workers have been constituting a growing fraction of the labour force. These groups are more mobile in employment than other workers, entering and leaving the labour market, shifting more frequently between jobs. As a result, they tend to experience higher average rates of unemployment. Second, unemployment insurance and other forms of assistance to unemployed persons have been made available to more categories of workers, and have become more generous in duration and amount. Workers who lose their jobs are under less pressure to look for other work, will tend to wait longer in the hope, generally fulfilled, of being re-called to their former employment, and can be more selective in the alternatives they consider. Further, the availability of unemployment insurance makes it more attractive to enter the labour force in the first place, and so may itself have stimulated the growth that has occurred in the labour force as a percentage of the population and also its changing composition.

The determinants of the natural rate of unemployment deserve much fuller analysis for both the United States and other countries. So also do the meaning of the recorded unemployment figures and the relation between the recorded figures and the natural rate. These issues are all of the utmost importance for public policy. However, they are side issues for my present limited purpose.

The connection between the state of employment and the level of efficiency or productivity of an economy is another topic that is of fundamental importance for public policy but is a side issue for my present purpose. There is a tendency to take it for granted that a high level of recorded unemployment is evidence of inefficient use of resources and conversely. This view is seriously in error. A low level of unemployment may be a sign of a forced-draft economy that is using its resources inefficiently and is inducing workers to sacrifice leisure for goods that they value less highly than the leisure under the mistaken belief that their real wages will be higher than they prove to be. Or a low natural rate of unemployment may reflect institutional arrangements that inhibit change. A highly static rigid economy may have a fixed place for everyone whereas a dynamic, highly progressive economy, which offers ever-changing opportunities and fosters flexibility, may have a high natural rate of unemployment. To illustrate how the same rate may correspond to very different conditions: both Japan and the United Kingdom had low average rates of unemployment from, say, 1950 to 1970, but Japan experienced rapid growth, the UK, stagnation.

The 'natural-rate' or 'accelerationist' or 'expectations-adjusted Phillips curve' hypothesis – as it has been variously designated – is by now widely accepted by economists, though by no means universally. A few still cling to the original Phillips curve; more recognise the difference between short-run and long-run curves but regard even the long-run curve as negatively sloped, though more steeply so than the short-run curves; some substitute a stable relation between the acceleration of inflation and unemployment for a stable relation between inflation and unemployment – aware of, but not concerned about, the possibility that the same logic that drove them to a second derivative will drive them to ever higher derivatives.

Much current economic research is devoted to exploring various aspects of this second stage – the dynamics of the process, the formation of expectations, and the kind of systematic policy, if any, that can have a predictable effect on real magnitudes. We can expect rapid progress on these issues. (Special mention should be made of the work on 'rational expectations', especially the seminal contributions of John Muth, Robert Lucas, and Thomas Sargent.) [Gordon (9).]

IV

STAGE 3: A POSITIVELY SLOPED PHILLIPS CURVE?

ALTHOUGH THE second stage is far from having been fully explored, let alone fully absorbed into the economic literature, the course of events is already producing a move to a third stage. In recent years, higher inflation has often been accompanied by higher not lower unemployment, especially for periods of several years in length. A simple statistical Phillips curve for such periods seems to be positively sloped, not vertical. The third stage is directed at accommodating this apparent empirical phenomenon. To do so, I suspect that it will have to include in the analysis the interdependence of economic experience and political developments. It will have to treat at least some political phenomena not as independent variables – as exogenous variables in econometric jargon – but as themselves determined by economic events – as endogenous variables [Gordon (8)]. The second stage was greatly influenced by two major developments in economic theory of the past few decades – one, the analysis of imperfect information and of the cost of acquiring information, pioneered by George Stigler; the other, the role of human capital in determining the form of labour contracts, pioneered by Gary Becker. The third stage will, I believe, be greatly influenced by a third major development – the application of economic analysis to political behaviour, a field in which pioneering work has also been done by Stigler and Becker as well as by Kenneth Arrow, Duncan Black, Anthony Downs, James Buchanan, Gordon Tullock, and others.

The apparent positive relation between inflation and unemployment has been a source of great concern to government policy-makers. Let me quote from a recent speech by Prime Minister Callaghan of Great Britain:

'We used to think that you could spend your way out of a recession, and increase employment by cutting taxes and boosting Government spending. I tell you, in all candour, that that option no longer exists, and that, insofar as it ever did exist, it only worked by . . . injecting bigger doses of inflation into the economy, followed by higher levels of unemployment as the next step. . . . That is the history of the past 20 years'. (Speech to Labour Party Conference, 28 September 1976.)

[17]

The same view is expressed in a Canadian Government white paper:

'Continuing inflation, particularly in North America, has been accompanied by an increase in measured unemployment rates.' ('The Way Ahead: A Framework for Discussion', Government of Canada Working Paper, October 1976.)

These are remarkable statements, running as they do directly counter to the policies adopted by almost every Western government throughout the post-war period.

(a) *Some evidence*

More systematic evidence for the past two decades is given in Table 1 and Figures 3 and 4, which show the rates of inflation and unemployment in seven industrialised countries over the past two

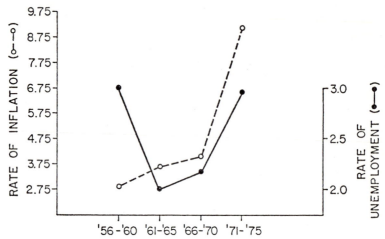

FIGURE 3: RATES OF UNEMPLOYMENT AND INFLATION, 1956 TO 1975, BY QUINQUENNIA: UNWEIGHTED AVERAGE FOR SEVEN COUNTRIES.

decades. According to the five-year averages in Table 1, the rate of inflation and the level of unemployment moved in opposite directions – the expected simple Phillips curve outcome – in five out of seven countries between the first two quinquennia (1956–60, 1961–65); in only four out of seven countries between the second and third quinquennia (1961–65 and 1966–70); and in only one of

[18]

TABLE I

Inflation and unemployment in seven countries, 1956 to 1975: Average values for successive quinquennia

DP = Rate of price change, per cent per year
U = Unemployment, percentage of labour force

	France		Germany		Italy		Japan		Sweden		United Kingdom		United States		Unweighted Average	
	DP	U	DP	U	DP	U	DP	U	DP	U	DP	U	DP	U	DP	U
1956 through 1960	5.6	1.1	1.8	2.9	1.9	6.7	1.9	1.4	3.7	1.9	2.6	1.5	2.0	5.2	2.8	3.0
1961 through 1965	3.7	1.2	2.8	0.7	4.9	3.1	6.2	0.9	3.6	1.2	3.5	1.6	1.3	5.5	3.7	2.0
1966 through 1970	4.4	1.7	2.4	1.2	3.0	3.5	5.4	1.1	4.6	1.6	4.6	2.1	4.2	3.9	4.1	2.2
1971 through 1975	8.8	2.5	6.1	2.1	11.3	3.3	11.4	1.4	7.9	1.8	13.0	3.2	6.7	6.1	9.3	2.9

Note: DP is rate of change of consumer prices compounded annually from calendar year 1955 to 1960; 1960 to 1965; 1965 to 1970; 1970 to 1975. U is average unemployment during five indicated calendar years. As a result, DP is dated one-half year prior to associated U.

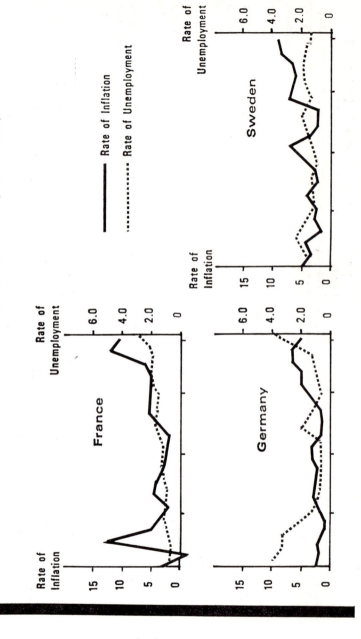

FIGURE 4:

INFLATION AND UNEMPLOYMENT IN SEVEN COUNTRIES, ANNUALLY, 1956 TO 1975

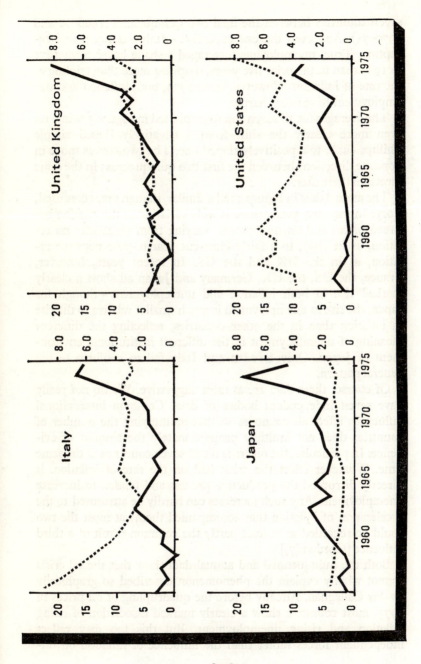

seven countries between the final two quinquennia (1966–70 and 1970–75). And even the one exception – Italy – is not a real exception. True, unemployment averaged a shade lower from 1971 to 1975 than in the prior five years, despite a more than tripling of the rate of inflation. However, since 1973, both inflation and unemployment have risen sharply.

The averages for all seven countries plotted in Figure 3 bring out even more clearly the shift from a negatively sloped simple Phillips curve to a positively sloped one. The two curves move in opposite directions between the first two quinquennia; in the same direction thereafter.

The annual data in Figure 4 tell a similar, though more confused, story. In the early years, there is wide variation in the relation between prices and unemployment, varying from essentially no relation, as in Italy, to a fairly clear-cut year-to-year negative relation, as in the UK and the US. In recent years, however, France, the US, the UK, Germany and Japan all show a clearly marked rise in both inflation and unemployment – though for Japan, the rise in unemployment is much smaller relative to the rise in inflation than in the other countries, reflecting the different meaning of unemployment in the different institutional environment of Japan. Only Sweden and Italy fail to conform to the general pattern.

Of course, these data are at most suggestive. We do not really have seven independent bodies of data. Common international influences affect all countries so that multiplying the number of countries does not multiply proportionately the amount of evidence. In particular, the oil crisis hit all seven countries at the same time. Whatever effect the crisis had on the rate of inflation, it directly disrupted the productive process and tended to increase unemployment. Any such increases can hardly be attributed to the acceleration of inflation that accompanied them; at most the two could be regarded as at least partly the common result of a third influence [Gordon (7)].

Both the quinquennial and annual data show that the oil crisis cannot wholly explain the phenomenon described so graphically by Mr Callaghan. Already before the quadrupling of oil prices in 1973, most countries show a clearly marked association of rising inflation and rising unemployment. But this too may reflect independent forces rather than the influence of inflation on un-

[22]

employment. For example, the same forces that have been raising the natural rate of unemployment in the US may have been operating in other countries and may account for their rising trend of unemployment, independently of the consequences of inflation.

Despite these qualifications, the data strongly suggest that, at least in some countries, of which Britain, Canada, and Italy may be the best examples, rising inflation and rising unemployment have been mutually reinforcing, rather than the separate effects of separate causes. The data are not inconsistent with the stronger statement that, in all industrialised countries, higher rates of inflation have some effects that, at least for a time, make for higher unemployment. The rest of this paper is devoted to a preliminary exploration of what some of these effects may be.

(b) *A tentative hypothesis*
I conjecture that a modest elaboration of the natural-rate hypothesis is all that is required to account for a positive relation between inflation and unemployment, though of course such a positive relation may also occur for other reasons. Just as the natural-rate hypothesis explains a negatively sloped Phillips curve over short periods as a temporary phenomenon that will disappear as economic agents adjust their expectations to reality, so a positively sloped Phillips curve over somewhat longer periods may occur as a transitional phenomenon that will disappear as economic agents adjust not only their expectations but their institutional and political arrangements to a new reality. When this is achieved, I believe that – as the natural-rate hypothesis suggests – the rate of unemployment will be largely independent of the average rate of inflation, though the efficiency of utilisation of resources may not be. High inflation need not mean either abnormally high or abnormally low unemployment. However, the institutional and political arrangements that accompany it, either as relics of earlier history or as products of the inflation itself, are likely to prove antithetical to the most productive use of employed resources – a special case of the distinction between the state of employment and the productivity of an economy referred to earlier.

Experience in many Latin American countries that have adjusted to chronically high inflation rates – experience that has been analysed most perceptively by some of my colleagues, particularly

Arnold Harberger and Larry Sjaastad [(12), (25)] – is consistent, I believe, with this view.

In the version of the natural-rate hypothesis summarised in Figure 2, the vertical curve is for alternative rates of fully anticipated inflation. Whatever that rate – be it negative, zero or positive – it can be built into every decision if it is fully anticipated. At an anticipated 20 per cent per year inflation, for example, long-term wage contracts would provide for a wage in each year that would rise relative to the zero-inflation wage by just 20 per cent per year; long-term loans would bear an interest rate 20 percentage points higher than the zero-inflation rate, or a principal that would be raised by 20 per cent a year; and so on – in short, the equivalent of a full indexing of all contracts. The high rate of inflation would have some real effects, by altering desired cash balances, for example, but it need not alter the efficiency of labour markets, or the length or terms of labour contracts, and hence, it need not change the natural rate of unemployment.

This analysis implicitly supposes, first, that inflation is steady or at least no more variable at a high rate than at a low – otherwise, it is unlikely that inflation would be as fully anticipated at high as at low rates of inflation; second, that the inflation is, or can be, open, with all prices free to adjust to the higher rate, so that relative price adjustments are the same with a 20 per cent inflation as with a zero inflation; third, really a variant of the second point, that there are no obstacles to indexing of contracts.

Ultimately, if inflation at an average rate of 20 per cent per year were to prevail for many decades, these requirements could come fairly close to being met, which is why I am inclined to retain the long-long-run vertical Phillips curve. But when a country initially moves to higher rates of inflation, these requirements will be systematically departed from. And such a transitional period may well extend over decades.

Consider, in particular, the US and the UK. For two centuries before World War II for the UK, and a century and a half for the US, prices varied about a roughly constant level, showing substantial increases in time of war, then post-war declines to roughly pre-war levels. The concept of a 'normal' price level was deeply embedded in the financial and other institutions of the two countries and in the habits and attitudes of their citizens.

In the immediate post-World War II period, prior experience

was widely expected to recur. The fact was post-war inflation superimposed on wartime inflation; yet the expectation in both the US and the UK was deflation. It took a long time for the fear of post-war deflation to dissipate – if it still has – and still longer before expectations started to adjust to the fundamental change in the monetary system. That adjustment is still far from complete [Klein (16)].

Indeed, we do not know what a complete adjustment will consist of. We cannot know now whether the industrialised countries will return to the pre-World War II pattern of a long-term stable price level, or will move toward the Latin American pattern of chronically high inflation rates – with every now and then an acute outbreak of super- or hyper-inflation, as occurred recently in Chile and Argentina [Harberger (11)] – or will undergo more radical economic and political change leading to a still different resolution of the present ambiguous situation.

This uncertainty – or more precisely, the circumstances producing this uncertainty – leads to systematic departures from the conditions required for a vertical Phillips curve.

The most fundamental departure is that a high inflation rate is not likely to be steady during the transition decades. Rather, the higher the rate, the more variable it is likely to be. That has been empirically true of differences among countries in the past several decades [Jaffe and Kleiman (14); Logue and Willett (17)]. It is also highly plausible on theoretical grounds – both about actual inflation and, even more clearly, the anticipations of economic agents with respect to inflation. Governments have not produced high inflation as a deliberate announced policy but as a consequence of other policies – in particular, policies of full employment and welfare state policies raising government spending. They all proclaim their adherence to the goal of stable prices. They do so in response to their constituents, who may welcome many of the side-effects of inflation, but are still wedded to the concept of stable money. A burst of inflation produces strong pressure to counter it. Policy goes from one direction to the other, encouraging wide variation in the actual and anticipated rate of inflation. And, of course, in such an environment, no one has single-valued anticipations. Everyone recognises that there is great uncertainty about what actual inflation will turn out to be over any specific future interval [Jaffe and Kleiman (14); Meiselman (20)].

[25]

The tendency for inflation that is high on the average to be highly variable is reinforced by the effect of inflation on the political cohesiveness of a country in which institutional arrangements and financial contracts have been adjusted to a long-term 'normal' price level. Some groups gain (e.g., home owners); others lose (e.g., owners of savings accounts and fixed interest securities). 'Prudent' behaviour becomes in fact reckless, and 'reckless' behaviour in fact prudent. The society is polarised; one group is set against another. Political unrest increases. The capacity of any government to govern is reduced at the same time that the pressure for strong action grows.

An increased variability of actual or anticipated inflation may raise the natural rate of unemployment in two rather different ways.

First, increased volatility shortens the optimum length of unindexed commitments and renders indexing more advantageous [Gray (10)]. But it takes time for actual practice to adjust. In the meantime, prior arrangements introduce rigidities that reduce the effectiveness of markets. An additional element of uncertainty is, as it were, added to every market arrangement. In addition, indexing is, even at best, an imperfect substitute for stability of the inflation rate. Price indexes are imperfect; they are available only with a lag, and generally are applied to contract terms only with a further lag.

These developments clearly lower economic efficiency. It is less clear what their effect is on recorded unemployment. High average inventories of all kinds is one way to meet increased rigidity and uncertainty. But that may mean labour-hoarding by enterprises and low unemployment or a larger force of workers between jobs and so high unemployment. Shorter commitments may mean more rapid adjustment of employment to changed conditions and so low unemployment, or the delay in adjusting the length of commitments may lead to less satisfactory adjustment and so high unemployment. Clearly, much additional research is necessary in this area to clarify the relative importance of the various effects. About all one can say now is that the slow adjustment of commitments and the imperfections of indexing may contribute to the recorded increase in unemployment.

A second related effect of increased volatility of inflation is to render market prices a less efficient system for co-ordinating economic activity. A fundamental function of a price system, as Hayek (13) emphasised so brilliantly, is to transmit compactly, efficiently, and at low cost the information that economic agents need in order to decide what to produce and how to produce it, or how to employ owned resources. The relevant information is about *relative* prices – of one product relative to another, of the services of one factor of production relative to another, of products relative to factor services, of prices now relative to prices in the future. But the information in practice is transmitted in the form of *absolute* prices – prices in dollars or pounds or kronor. If the price level is on the average stable or changing at a steady rate, it is relatively easy to extract the signal about relative prices from the observed absolute prices. The more volatile the rate of general inflation, the harder it becomes to extract the signal about relative prices from the absolute prices: the broadcast about relative prices is as it were being jammed by the noise coming from the inflation broadcast [Lucas (18), (19); Harberger (11)]. At the extreme, the system of absolute prices becomes nearly useless, and economic agents resort either to an alternative currency, or to barter, with disastrous effects on productivity.

Again, the effect on economic efficiency is clear, on unemployment less so. But, again, it seems plausible that the average level of unemployment would be raised by the increased amount of noise in market signals, at least during the period when institutional arrangements are not yet adapted to the new situation.

These effects of increased volatility of inflation would occur even if prices were legally free to adjust – if, in that sense, the inflation were open. In practice, the distorting effects of uncertainty, rigidity of voluntary long-term contracts, and the contamination of price signals will almost certainly be reinforced by legal restrictions on price change. In the modern world, governments are themselves producers of services sold on the market: from postal services to a wide range of other items. Other prices are regulated by government, and require government approval for change: from air fares to taxicab fares to charges for electricity. In these cases, governments cannot avoid being involved in the price-fixing process. In addition, the social and political forces unleashed by volatile inflation rates will lead governments to try to repress inflation in still other areas: by explicit price and wage control, or by pressuring private businesses or unions 'voluntarily' to exercise 'restraint', or by speculating in foreign exchange in order to alter the exchange rate.

The details will vary from time to time and from country to country, but the general result is the same: reduction in the capacity of the price system to guide economic activity; distortions in relative prices because of the introduction of greater friction, as it were, in all markets; and, very likely, a higher recorded rate of unemployment [(5)].

The forces I have just described may render the political and economic system dynamically unstable and produce hyper-inflation and radical political change – as in many defeated countries after World War I, or in Chile and Argentina more recently. At the other extreme, before any such catastrophe occurs, policies may be adopted that will achieve a relatively low and stable rate of inflation and lead to the dismantling of many of the interferences with the price system. That would re-establish the preconditions for the straightforward natural-rate hypothesis and enable that hypothesis to be used to predict the course of the transition.

An intermediate possibility is that the system will reach stability at a fairly constant though high average rate of inflation. In that case, unemployment should also settle down to a fairly constant level decidedly lower than during the transition. As the preceding discussion emphasises, *increasing* volatility and *increasing* government intervention with the price system are the major factors that seem likely to raise unemployment, not *high* volatility or a *high* level of intervention.

Ways of coping with both volatility and intervention will develop: through indexing and similar arrangements for coping with volatility of inflation; through the development of indirect ways of altering prices and wages for avoiding government controls.

Under these circumstances, the long-run Phillips curve would again be vertical, and we would be back at the natural-rate hypothesis, though perhaps for a different range of inflation rates than that for which it was first suggested.

Because the phenomenon to be explained is the co-existence of high inflation and high unemployment, I have stressed the effect of institutional changes produced by a transition from a monetary system in which there was a 'normal' price level to a monetary

[28]

system consistent with long periods of high, and possibly highly variable, inflation. It should be noted that once these institutional changes were made, and economic agents had adjusted their practices and anticipations to them, a reversal to the earlier monetary framework or even the adoption in the new monetary framework of a successful policy of low inflation would in its turn require new adjustments, and these might have many of the same adverse transitional effects on the level of employment. There would appear to be an intermediate-run negatively sloped Phillips curve instead of the positively sloped one I have tried to rationalise.

V

CONCLUSION

ONE CONSEQUENCE of the Keynesian revolution of the 1930s was the acceptance of a rigid absolute wage level, and a nearly rigid absolute price level, as a starting point for analysing short-term economic change. It came to be taken for granted that these were essentially institutional data and were so regarded by economic agents, so that changes in aggregate nominal demand would be reflected almost entirely in output and hardly at all in prices. The age-old confusion between absolute prices and relative prices gained a new lease on life.

In this intellectual atmosphere it was understandable that economists would analyse the relation between unemployment and *nominal* rather than *real* wages and would implicitly regard changes in anticipated *nominal* wages as equal to changes in anticipated *real* wages. Moreover, the empirical evidence that initially suggested a stable relation between the level of unemployment and the rate of change of nominal wages was drawn from a period when, despite sharp short-period fluctuations in prices, there was a relatively stable long-run price level and when the expectation of continued stability was widely shared. Hence these data flashed no warning signals about the special character of the assumptions.

The hypothesis that there is a stable relation between the level of unemployment and the rate of inflation was adopted by the economics profession with alacrity. It filled a gap in Keynes's theoretical structure. It seemed to be the 'one equation' that

Keynes himself had said 'we are . . . short' (15). In addition, it seemed to provide a reliable tool for economic policy, enabling the economist to inform the policy-maker about the alternatives available to him.

As in any science, so long as experience seemed to be consistent with the reigning hypothesis, it continued to be accepted, although, as always, a few dissenters questioned its validity.

But as the 1950s turned into the 1960s, and the 1960s into the 1970s, it became increasingly difficult to accept the hypothesis in its simple form. It seemed to take larger and larger doses of inflation to keep down the level of unemployment. Stagflation reared its ugly head.

Many attempts were made to patch up the hypothesis by allowing for special factors such as the strength of trade unions. But experience stubbornly refused to conform to the patched-up version.

A more radical revision was required. It took the form of stressing the importance of surprises – of differences between actual and anticipated magnitudes. It restored the primacy of the distinction between 'real' and 'nominal' magnitudes. There is a 'natural rate of unemployment' at any time determined by real factors. This natural rate will tend to be attained when expectations are on the average realised. The same real situation is consistent with any absolute level of prices or of price change, provided allowance is made for the effect of price change on the real cost of holding money balances. In this respect, money is neutral. On the other hand, unanticipated changes in aggregate nominal demand and in inflation will cause systematic errors of perception on the part of employers and employees alike that will initially lead unemployment to deviate in the opposite direction from its natural rate. In this respect, money is not neutral. However, such deviations are transitory, though it may take a long chronological time before they are reversed and finally eliminated as anticipations adjust.

The natural-rate hypothesis contains the original Phillips curve hypothesis as a special case and rationalises a far broader range of experience, in particular the phenomenon of stagflation. It has by now been widely though not universally accepted.

However, the natural-rate hypothesis in its present form has not proved rich enough to explain a more recent development – a

[30]

move from stagflation to slumpflation. In recent years, higher inflation has often been accompanied by higher unemployment – not lower unemployment, as the simple Phillips curve would suggest, nor the same unemployment, as the natural-rate hypothesis would suggest.

This recent association of higher inflation with higher unemployment may reflect the common impact of such events as the oil crisis, or independent forces that have imparted a common upward trend to inflation and unemployment.

However, a major factor in some countries and a contributing factor in others may be that they are in a transitional period – this time to be measured by quinquennia or decades, not years. The public has not adapted its attitudes or its institutions to a new monetary environment. Inflation tends not only to be higher but also increasingly volatile and to be accompanied by widening government intervention into the setting of prices. The growing volatility of inflation and the growing departure of relative prices from the values that market forces alone would set combine to render the economic system less efficient, to introduce frictions in all markets, and, very likely, to raise the recorded rate of unemployment.

On this analysis, the present situation cannot last. It will either degenerate into hyper-inflation and radical change; or institutions will adjust to a situation of chronic inflation; or governments will adopt policies that will produce a low rate of inflation and less government intervention into the fixing of prices.

I have told a perfectly standard story of how scientific theories are revised. Yet it is a story that has far-reaching importance.

Government policy about inflation and unemployment has been at the centre of political controversy. Ideological war has raged over these matters. Yet the drastic change that has occurred in economic theory has not been a result of ideological warfare. It has not resulted from divergent political beliefs or aims. It has responded almost entirely to the force of events: brute experience proved far more potent than the strongest of political or ideological preferences.

The importance for humanity of a correct understanding of positive economic science is vividly brought out by a statement made nearly two hundred years ago by Pierre S. du Pont, a Deputy from Nemours to the French National Assembly, speaking, appropriately enough, on a proposal to issue additional *assignats* – the fiat money of the French Revolution:

'Gentlemen, it is a disagreeable custom to which one is too easily led by the harshness of the discussions, to assume evil intentions. It is necessary to be gracious as to intentions; one should believe them good, and apparently they are; but we do not have to be gracious at all to inconsistent logic or to absurd reasoning. Bad logicians have committed more involuntary crimes than bad men have done intentionally.' (25 September 1790.)

References

(1) Milton Friedman, 'The Methodology of Positive Economics', *Essays in Positive Economics* (Chicago: University of Chicago Press, 1953).

(2) —, 'What Price Guideposts?', in G. P. Shultz and R. Z. Aliber (eds.), *Guidelines: Informal Contracts and the Market Place* (Chicago: University of Chicago Press, 1966), pp. 17–39 and 55–61.

(3) —, 'An Inflationary Recession', *Newsweek*, 17 October, 1966.

(4) —, 'The Role of Monetary Policy', *American Economic Review*, 58 (March 1968), pp. 1–17.

(5) —, *Price Theory* (Chicago: Aldine Publishing Co., 1976), ch. 12.

(6) —, *Inflation: Causes and Consequences* (Bombay: Asia Publishing House, 1963), reprinted in *Dollars and Deficits* (Englewood Cliffs, N.J.: Prentice-Hall, 1968), pp. 21–71.

(7) Robert J. Gordon, 'Alternative Responses of Policy to External Supply Shocks', *Brookings Papers on Economic Activity*, No. 1 (1975), pp. 183–206.

(8) —, 'The Demand and Supply of Inflation', *Journal of Law and Economics*, 18 (December 1975), pp. 807–836.

(9) —, 'Recent Developments in the Theory of Inflation and Unemployment', *Journal of Monetary Economics*, 2 (1976), pp. 185–219.

(10) Jo Anna Gray, 'Essays on Wage Indexation', unpublished Ph.D. dissertation, University of Chicago, 1976.

(11) Arnold C. Harberger, 'Inflation', *The Great Ideas Today, 1976* (Chicago: Encyclopaedia Britannica, Inc., 1976), pp. 95–106.

(12) —, 'The Inflation Problem in Latin America', a report prepared for the Buenos Aires (March 1966) meeting of the Inter-American Committee of the Alliance for Progress, published in Spanish as 'El problema de la inflación en América Latina', in Centro de Estudios Monetarios Latinoamericanos, *Boletin Mensual*, June 1966, pp. 253–269; reprinted in Economic Development Institute, *Trabajos sobre desarrollo económico* (Washington, D.C.: IBRD, 1967).

(13) F. A. Hayek, 'The Use of Knowledge in Society', *American Economic Review*, 35 (September 1945), pp. 519–530.

(14) Dwight Jaffe and Ephraim Kleiman, 'The Welfare Implications of Uneven Inflation', Seminar paper No. 50, Institute for International Economic Studies, University of Stockholm, November 1975.

(15) J. M. Keynes, *General Theory of Employment, Interest, and Money* (London: Macmillan, 1936), p. 276.

(16) Benjamin Klein, 'Our New Monetary Standard: The Measurement and Effects of Price Uncertainty, 1880–1973', *Economic Inquiry*, December 1975, pp. 461–483.

(17) Dennis E. Logue and Thomas D. Willett, 'A Note on the Relation between the Rate and Variability of Inflation', *Economica*, May 1976, pp. 151–158.

(18) Robert E. Lucas, 'Some International Evidence on Output-Inflation Tradeoffs', *American Economic Review*, 63 (June 1973), pp. 326–334.

(19) —, 'An Equilibrium Model of the Business Cycle', *Journal of Political Economy*, 83 (December 1975), pp. 1,113–1,144.

(20) David Meiselman, 'Capital Formation, Monetary and Financial Adjustments', *Proceedings*, 27th National Conference of Tax Foundation, 1976, pp. 9–15.

(21) John Muth, 'Rational Expectations and the Theory of Price Movements', *Econometrica*, 29 (July 1961), pp. 315–333.

(22) E. S. Phelps, 'Phillips Curve, Expectations of Inflation and Optimal Unemployment Over Time', *Economica*, 34 (August 1967), pp. 254–281.

(23) —, 'Money Wage Dynamics and Labour Market Equilibrium', in E. S. Phelps (ed.), *Microeconomic Foundations of Employment and Inflation Theory* (New York: Norton, 1970).

(24) A. W. Phillips 'The Relationship between Unemployment and the Rate of Change of Money Wage Rates in the United Kingdom, 1861–1957', *Economica*, November 1958, pp. 283–299.

(25) Larry A. Sjaastad, 'Monetary Policy and Suppressed Inflation in Latin America', in R. Z. Aliber (ed.), *National Monetary Policies and the International Financial System* (Chicago: University of Chicago Press, 1974), pp. 127–138.

Professor Friedman's
Principal Writings

Essays in Positive Economics, The University of Chicago Press, 1953.

Studies in the Quantity Theory of Money, The University of Chicago Press, 1956.

A Theory of the Consumption Function, Princeton University Press, Princeton, New Jersey, 1957.

A Program for Monetary Stability, Fordham University Press, New York, 1959.

Capitalism and Freedom, The University of Chicago Press, 1962.

Price Theory, Aldine Publishing, Chicago, 1962.

A Monetary History of the United States, 1867–1960, Princeton University Press, Princeton, New Jersey, 1963.

Dollars and Deficits, Prentice-Hall, New Jersey, 1968.

The Optimum Quantity of Money, Aldine Publishing, Chicago, 1969.

An Economist's Protest, Thomas Horton, New Jersey, 1972.

Milton Friedman's Monetary Framework, The University of Chicago Press, 1976.

[continued from inside back cover]

anticipated inflation. Gainers and losers are polarised. Pressure for government action against inflation is frustrated at the time when there is increasing difficulty in governing.

14. Increasingly (rather than highly) volatile inflation may raise the natural rate of unemployment: first, because of slower market adjustment and the imperfections of indexing, and, second, because relative market prices are distorted and so transmit information and co-ordinate economic activity less efficiently. There may be escape to barter or to an external currency.

15. After a time these tendencies may produce political and economic instability, hyper-inflation, and political revolution. Or there may be measures to obtain a low and stable rate of inflation and so make possible a dismantling of price regulations. Or there may be the intermediate possibility of economic stability with fairly constant but high inflation.

16. Indexing could be developed to cope with volatile inflation, and indirect alteration in prices (including wages) could be developed to avoid government controls. Unemployment could again be independent of inflation : the long-run Phillips Curve is again vertical.

17. The former Keynesian remedy for unemployment – inflation – has now been accepted in Britain (and in Canada) as erroneous. 'We used to think you could spend your way out of a recession . . . that option no longer exists . . . in so far as it ever did . . . it worked by injecting bigger doses of inflation . . . followed by higher levels of unemployment . . . That is the history of the past 20 years' (Mr James Callaghan, September 1976).

18. Such change in economic thinking on the relationship between inflation and unemployment, and on governmental policy designed to control them, has resulted not from political preferences but from the testing of hypotheses and incorporation of the results into positive economic analysis. The errors have been caused not by evil economists or politicians but by bad economics.